First Atlas

This book belongs to

_____

Rand McNally
for
Kids™

CONTENTS

Published by Rand McNally in 1994 in the U.S.A.

First published in 1993 by
Kibworth Books
Imperial Road
Kibworth Beauchamp
Leicester LE8 0HR

Planned and produced by
Andromeda Oxford Limited
11-15 The Vineyard
Abingdon
Oxon OX14 3PX

Flags produced by Lovell Johns, Oxford, U.K. and authenticated by The Flag Research Center, Winchester, Mass. 01890 U.S.A.

Library of Congress Cataloging-in-Publication Data

Rand McNally and Company
        First atlas / illustrated by Claire Henley and Chris Russell/
        p. cm.
        ISBN 0-528-83679-X
        1. Children's atlases. [1. Atlases.] I. Henley, Claire, ill. II. Russell, Chris, ill. III Title.
G1021.R175 1994 <G&M>
912-dc20   93-37528
                              CIP
                            MAP AC

Printed in Italy by Graficom S.R.L.

Introduction

What Are Maps?

Maps are drawings that show us where things are and help us find our way around. When maps are put together in a book, the book is called an atlas. Some of the maps in this atlas show large areas of land called continents. Other maps show parts of continents and countries.

What Do Maps Show?

Maps in this atlas show continents, countries, cities, islands, forests, deserts, mountains, rivers, lakes, oceans, and seas. Pictures on the maps are called symbols and show many other things. The map symbols and other pictures and stories around the maps tell us a lot about the world. A part of each page tells more about the land, the weather, and the people.

The Land

You can read and learn about the plants, mountains, lakes, and rivers that are found in a place.

The Weather

You can read and learn about what the weather is like in different places.

The People

You can read and learn about the people who live in the countries.

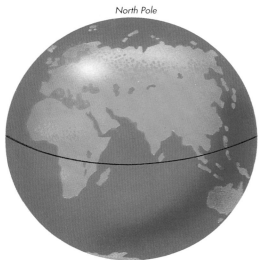

North Pole

South Pole

NORTH AMERICA
EUROPE
ASIA
AFRICA
SOUTH AMERICA
Equator
AUSTRALIA
ANTARCTICA

The Earth

The Earth is round like a ball. It spins in space like a giant top. It has a North Pole and a South Pole. There is an imaginary line drawn on maps that goes around the Earth halfway between the two Poles. This line is the Equator.

A Map of the World

To make maps we must show the Earth's surface as if it were flat. To do this is like peeling an orange and flattening the peel on a plate. Then the countries can be drawn on flat paper. The four-pointed symbol on the map shows direction. It points north (N), south (S), east (E), and west (W). On the map above, the continent of Africa is north and west of Australia.

Symbols

Look here to see what the pictures on the maps mean. On the maps capital cities are shown by a large dot. Country boundaries are shown with a black line.

Natural Habitats

Farming

Resources and Industry

Mineral Ore | Gold Mining | Diamond Mining

Gas Rig | Oil Rig | Ship Building | Industry

Coniferous Forest | Tropical Areas | Mediterranean Woodlands | Rain Forest | Grassland

Tea | Wine | Sheep Farming | Pig Farming | Poultry Farming

Beef Cattle | Dairy Cattle | Grain Farming | Dairy Produce | Fishing | Potatoes

Apples | Corn | Rice | Peanuts | Sugar Cane | Logging

Paper Industry | Rubber | Cotton | Tobacco | Cocoa | Coffee

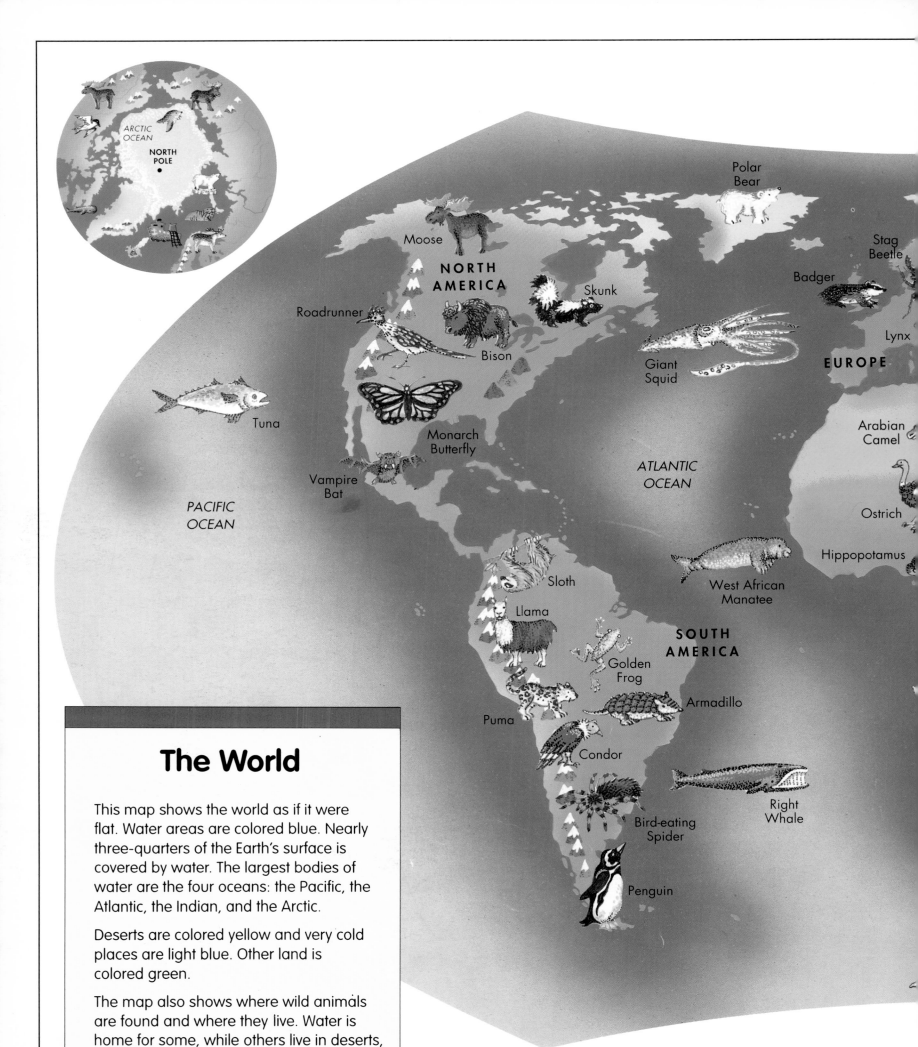

ARCTIC
OCEAN

NORTH
POLE

Polar
Bear

Moose

NORTH
AMERICA

Skunk

Stag
Beetle

Roadrunner

Badger

Bison

Giant
Squid

Lynx

EUROPE

Tuna

ATLANTIC
OCEAN

Arabian
Camel

PACIFIC
OCEAN

Monarch
Butterfly

Vampire
Bat

Ostrich

West African
Manatee

Hippopotamus

Sloth

Llama

SOUTH
AMERICA

Golden
Frog

Armadillo

Puma

Condor

Right
Whale

Bird-eating
Spider

Penguin

The World

This map shows the world as if it were
flat. Water areas are colored blue. Nearly
three-quarters of the Earth's surface is
covered by water. The largest bodies of
water are the four oceans: the Pacific, the
Atlantic, the Indian, and the Arctic.

Deserts are colored yellow and very cold
places are light blue. Other land is
colored green.

The map also shows where wild animals
are found and where they live. Water is
home for some, while others live in deserts,
mountains, or cold parts of the continents.

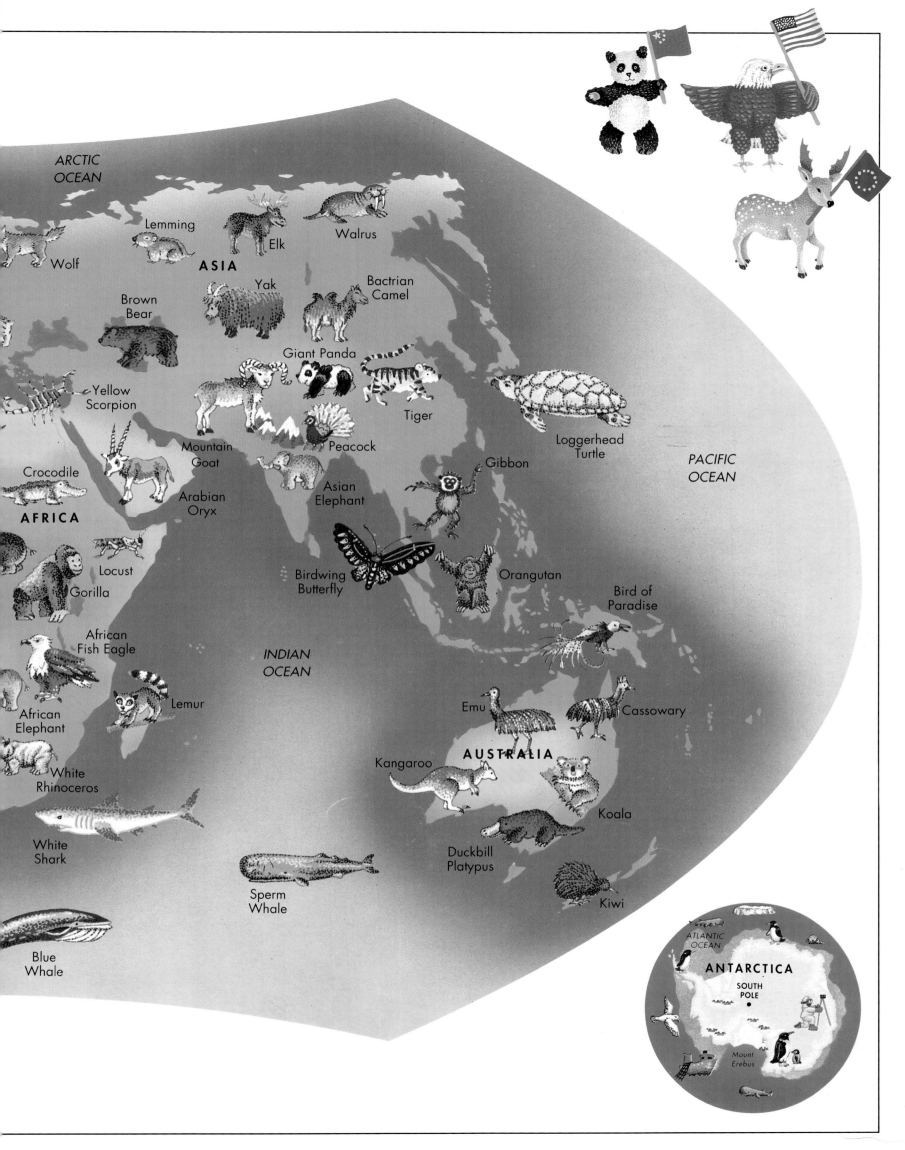

ARCTIC
OCEAN

Wolf

Lemming

Elk

Walrus

ASIA

Brown
Bear

Yak

Bactrian
Camel

Giant Panda

Yellow
Scorpion

Mountain
Goat

Tiger

Loggerhead
Turtle

Crocodile

Peacock

PACIFIC
OCEAN

AFRICA

Arabian
Oryx

Asian
Elephant

Gibbon

Locust

Birdwing
Butterfly

Gorilla

Orangutan

Bird of
Paradise

African
Fish Eagle

INDIAN
OCEAN

Lemur

Emu

Cassowary

African
Elephant

AUSTRALIA

White
Rhinoceros

Kangaroo

Koala

White
Shark

Duckbill
Platypus

Sperm
Whale

Kiwi

Blue
Whale

ATLANTIC
OCEAN

ANTARCTICA

SOUTH
POLE

Mount
Erebus

5

The United States, Mexico, and Middle America

Most of the United States lies between the Atlantic and Pacific Oceans, Canada and Mexico. Alaska, in the far north, and Hawaii, in the Pacific Ocean, are also parts of the United States. Middle America is between Mexico and South America, and includes countries in the Caribbean Sea.

The Land

High mountains cover most of the western United States. From these mountains to the Atlantic Ocean the land is lower and flatter. Mountains also cover much of Mexico and Middle America.

The Weather

Northern United States has snowy winters and warm summers. There are mild winters and hot summers in the south and long, cold winters in Alaska. Hawaii and Middle America are warm all year. The high parts of Mexico and western United States are very dry.

The People

Native Americans include the Navajo and Maya. About 500 years ago, people began coming from Europe. Most people in the United States speak English. Most people in Mexico speak Spanish.

| 250 | 500 | 750 | 1000 |

MILES

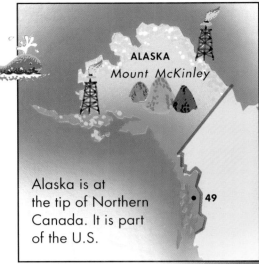

ALASKA
Mount McKinley

Alaska is at the tip of Northern Canada. It is part of the U.S.

• 49

Lights, Camera, Action!

Many American movies are made in the area around Los Angeles, California, especially in Hollywood. Some are made outdoors and some in huge studios with special effects.

50

HAWAII

The Hawaiian Islands are part of the U.S. They are in the Pacific Ocean.

N
W E
S

WASHINGTON
• 45

46 •

OREGON

• 44

IDAHO

Sierra Nevada

San Francisco

• 47   • 48   NEVADA

43

Golden Gate

UTAH

CALIFORNIA

Los Angeles •

Colorado River

42 •
ARIZONA

Surfer

PACIFIC OCEAN

Cactus

Ancient Stones

The Aztecs lived in Mexico over 500 years ago. They built stone pyramids and temples. Their capital stood where Mexico City is today.

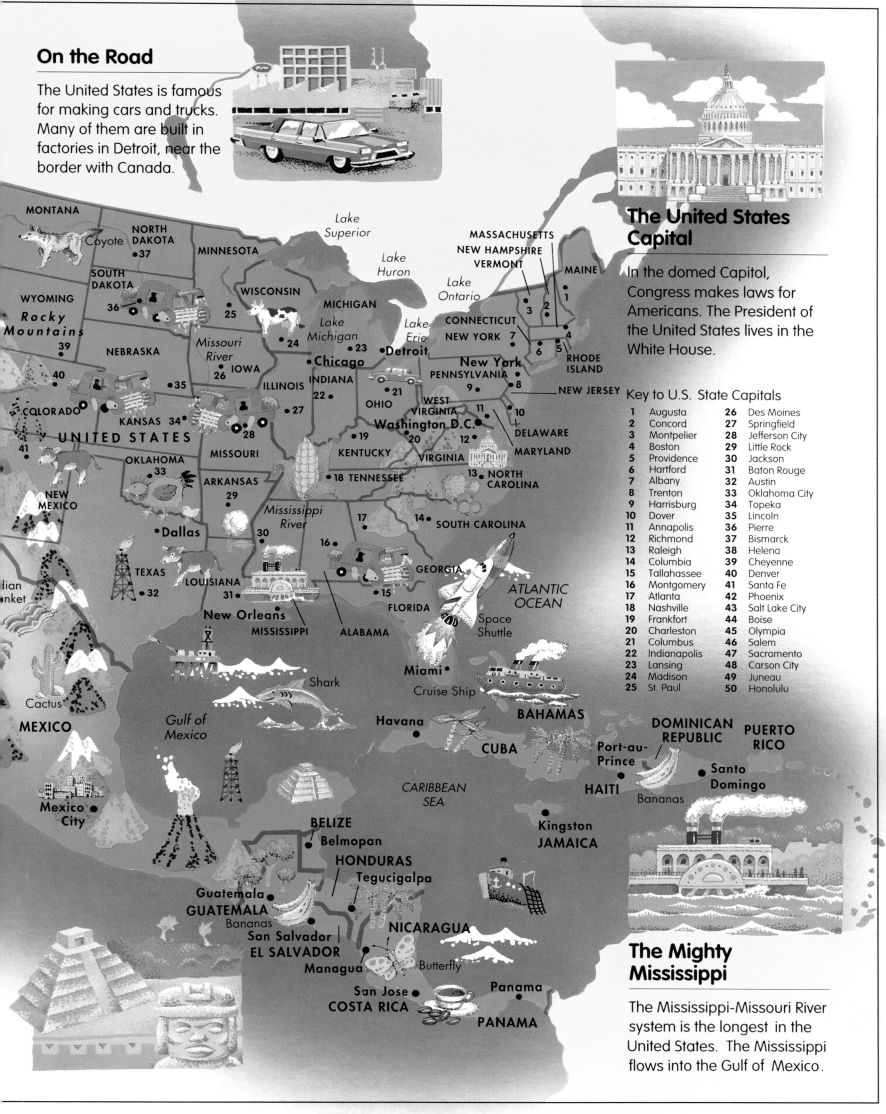

On the Road

The United States is famous for making cars and trucks. Many of them are built in factories in Detroit, near the border with Canada.

The United States Capital

In the domed Capitol, Congress makes laws for Americans. The President of the United States lives in the White House.

MONTANA
Coyote
NORTH DAKOTA
●37
MINNESOTA
Lake Superior
Lake Huron
MASSACHUSETTS
NEW HAMPSHIRE
VERMONT
MAINE
SOUTH DAKOTA
●36
WISCONSIN
MICHIGAN
Lake Ontario
3 2 1
CONNECTICUT
NEW YORK 7
WYOMING
Rocky Mountains
●39
●25
Lake Michigan
Lake Erie
6 5 4
RHODE ISLAND
NEBRASKA
Missouri River
●24
●23
Detroit
New York
PENNSYLVANIA
9
8
●40
IOWA
26
Chicago
INDIANA
22
OHIO
●21
NEW JERSEY
COLORADO
●35
ILLINOIS
●27
WEST VIRGINIA
11
10
DELAWARE
UNITED STATES
KANSAS 34 ●
●28
Washington D.C.
●19
20
12
MARYLAND
41
OKLAHOMA
●33
MISSOURI
KENTUCKY
VIRGINIA
13
NORTH CAROLINA
NEW MEXICO
ARKANSAS
29
●18 TENNESSEE
17
14
SOUTH CAROLINA
Indian blanket
Dallas
Mississippi River
30
16
GEORGIA
Cactus
TEXAS
●32
LOUISIANA
31
New Orleans
MISSISSIPPI
ALABAMA
●15
FLORIDA
ATLANTIC OCEAN
Space Shuttle
MEXICO
Gulf of Mexico
Shark
Miami
Cruise Ship
BAHAMAS
Mexico City
Havana
CUBA
CARIBBEAN SEA
DOMINICAN REPUBLIC
PUERTO RICO
Port-au-Prince
HAITI
Santo Domingo
Bananas
BELIZE
Belmopan
Kingston
JAMAICA
HONDURAS
Tegucigalpa
Guatemala
GUATEMALA
Bananas
NICARAGUA
San Salvador
EL SALVADOR
Managua
Butterfly
San Jose
COSTA RICA
Panama
PANAMA

Key to U.S. State Capitals

1	Augusta	26	Des Moines
2	Concord	27	Springfield
3	Montpelier	28	Jefferson City
4	Boston	29	Little Rock
5	Providence	30	Jackson
6	Hartford	31	Baton Rouge
7	Albany	32	Austin
8	Trenton	33	Oklahoma City
9	Harrisburg	34	Topeka
10	Dover	35	Lincoln
11	Annapolis	36	Pierre
12	Richmond	37	Bismarck
13	Raleigh	38	Helena
14	Columbia	39	Cheyenne
15	Tallahassee	40	Denver
16	Montgomery	41	Santa Fe
17	Atlanta	42	Phoenix
18	Nashville	43	Salt Lake City
19	Frankfort	44	Boise
20	Charleston	45	Olympia
21	Columbus	46	Salem
22	Indianapolis	47	Sacramento
23	Lansing	48	Carson City
24	Madison	49	Juneau
25	St. Paul	50	Honolulu

The Mighty Mississippi

The Mississippi-Missouri River system is the longest in the United States. The Mississippi flows into the Gulf of Mexico.

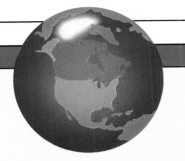

Canada

Canada lies between the Pacific Ocean, Alaska, the Arctic Ocean, the Atlantic Ocean, and the main part of the United States. Stretching almost to the North Pole, it is the world's second largest country. Canada is part of the continent of North America.

The Land

The Rocky Mountains tower above Canada's Pacific coast. Much of Canada is covered with rocks and forests. Near the North Pole, it is too cold for trees to grow. Near the United States are flat lands that are good for farming.

The Weather

Near the North Pole, Canada is very cold all year. Even the sea is frozen. Near the United States winters are cold and snowy, and summers are warm.

The People

Native people in Canada include the Inuit in the far north and other peoples of the forests. In the last four hundred years, people have come to Canada from Europe and Asia. Canada has two main languages, English and French.

250   500   750   1000

MILES

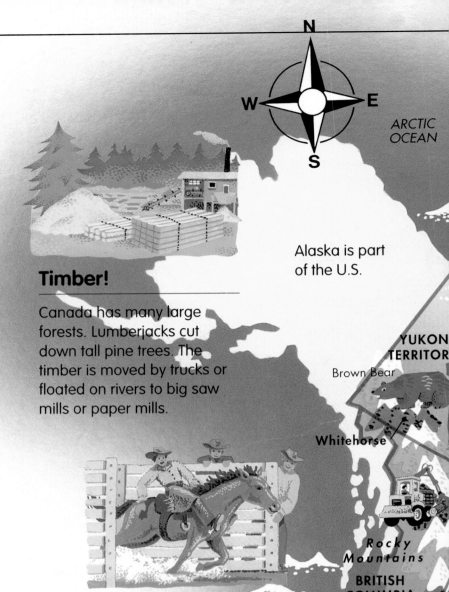

Timber!

Canada has many large forests. Lumberjacks cut down tall pine trees. The timber is moved by trucks or floated on rivers to big saw mills or paper mills.

Alaska is part of the U.S.

ARCTIC OCEAN

YUKON TERRITORY

Brown Bear

Whitehorse

Rocky Mountains

BRITISH COLUMBIA

PACIFIC OCEAN

Vancouver

Victoria

A Great Show at Calgary

Canadian cowboys hold an annual show to display their skills. It is called the Calgary Stampede for the city where it takes place. Cowboys rope cattle and ride bucking broncos.

Canada's Breadbasket

The central part of Canada is called the Prairies. On this flat land farmers raise huge fields of wheat. Much of this wheat is shipped to other countries.

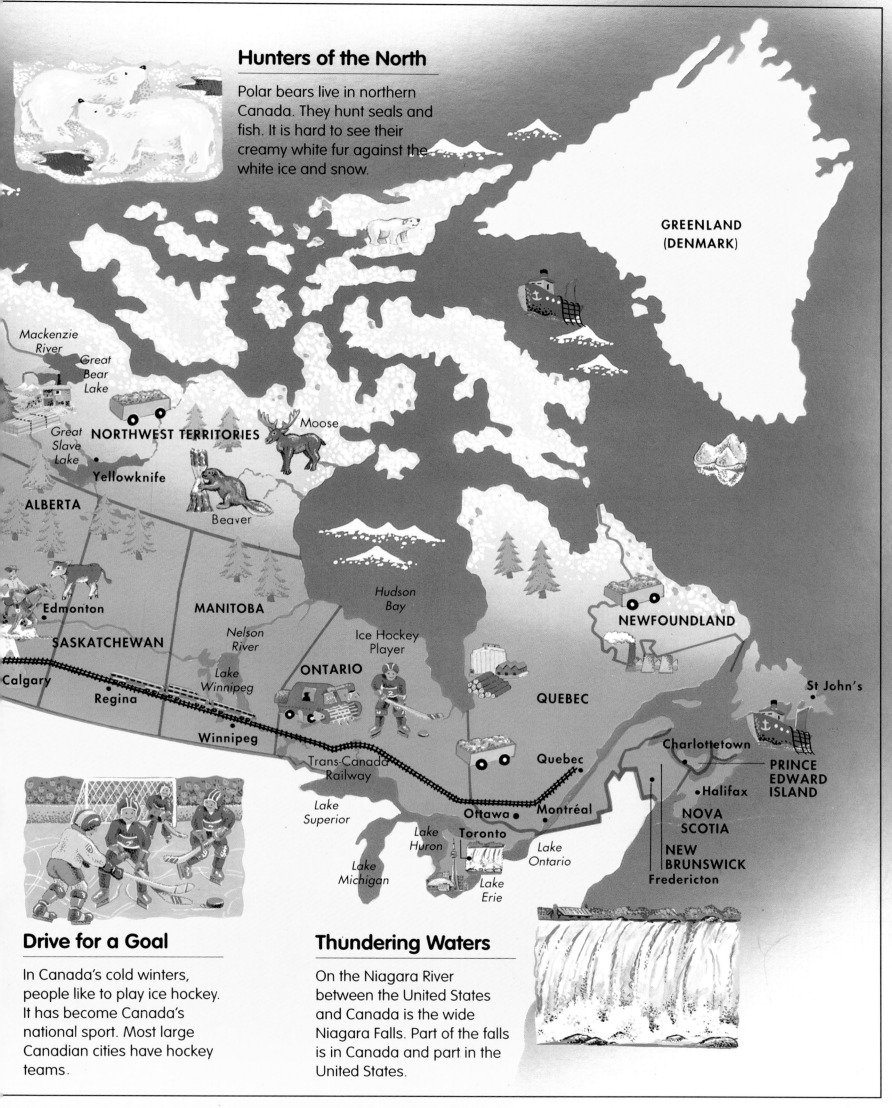

Hunters of the North

Polar bears live in northern Canada. They hunt seals and fish. It is hard to see their creamy white fur against the white ice and snow.

GREENLAND (DENMARK)

Mackenzie River

Great Bear Lake

NORTHWEST TERRITORIES

Great Slave Lake

• Yellowknife

Moose

Beaver

ALBERTA

• Edmonton

SASKATCHEWAN

MANITOBA

Nelson River

Lake Winnipeg

Hudson Bay

Ice Hockey Player

ONTARIO

NEWFOUNDLAND

Calgary

Regina

Winnipeg

QUEBEC

St John's

Trans-Canada Railway

Quebec

Charlottetown

PRINCE EDWARD ISLAND

Lake Superior

Ottawa

Montréal

• Halifax

Lake Huron

Toronto

Lake Ontario

NOVA SCOTIA

Lake Michigan

Lake Erie

NEW BRUNSWICK

Fredericton

Drive for a Goal

In Canada's cold winters, people like to play ice hockey. It has become Canada's national sport. Most large Canadian cities have hockey teams.

Thundering Waters

On the Niagara River between the United States and Canada is the wide Niagara Falls. Part of the falls is in Canada and part in the United States.

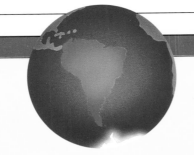

South America

There are 13 countries in South America. The largest is Brazil, and the smallest is French Guiana. A narrow strip of land joins Colombia to Central America. The far end of South America is Cape Horn.

The Land

South America has high mountains near the Pacific Ocean. In the valley of the Amazon River is the world's largest rain forest. Scientists worry that too many trees in the rain forest are being cut down. Other parts of South America are covered with grassy plains.

The Weather

It is hot and rainy around the Amazon River. Near Cape Horn it is cold and stormy.

The People

Native Americans have lived in South America for thousands of years. During the last 500 years, people from Europe, Africa, and Asia have come to South America to live. Most people in South America speak Spanish or Portuguese.

| 250 | 500 | 750 | 1000 |

MILES

Bogotá ●
COLOMB

Quito ●
ECUADOR

Llama

PERU

Lima ●

PACIFIC OCEAN

In the Rain Forest

The rain forests of South America are home to many plants and animals. There are many kinds of vines, flowers, trees, monkeys, and birds.

Long Ago in the Andes

The Incas lived in Peru more than 500 years ago. They built roads, bridges, and cities high in the mountains. Their capital city was Machu Picchu.

Cowboys of the South

Many herds of cattle are raised on the grasslands of Argentina. The cowboys who care for them are called gauchos (pronounced GOW-choz).

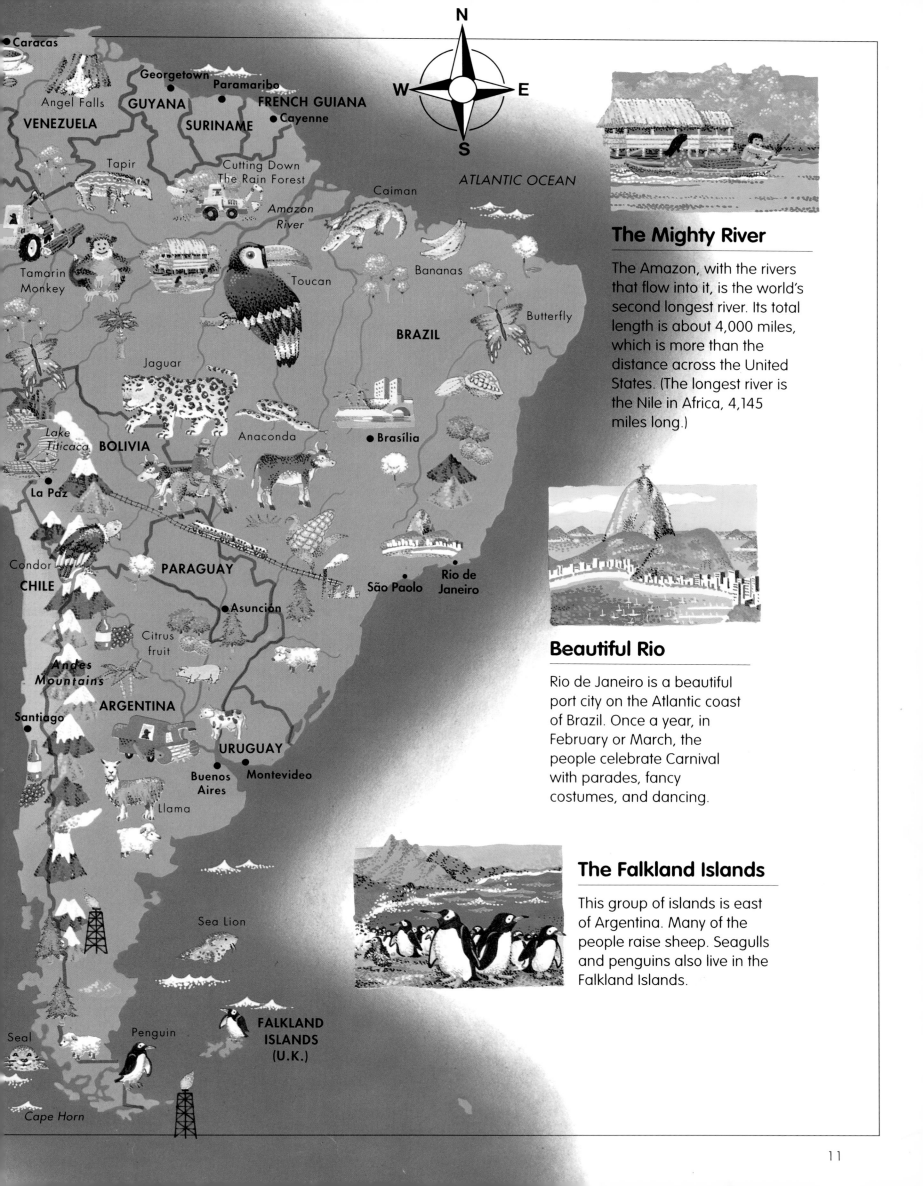

Caracas

Angel Falls
VENEZUELA

GUYANA
Georgetown

Paramaribo
FRENCH GUIANA
SURINAME
Cayenne

Tapir

Cutting Down
The Rain Forest

Amazon
River

Caiman

ATLANTIC OCEAN

Tamarin
Monkey

Toucan

Bananas

Butterfly

BRAZIL

Jaguar

Anaconda

Brasília

Lake
Titicaca
BOLIVIA

La Paz

Condor

São Paolo

Rio de
Janeiro

CHILE

PARAGUAY

Asunción

Citrus
fruit

*Andes
Mountains*

ARGENTINA

URUGUAY

**Buenos
Aires**
Montevideo

Llama

Santiago

Sea Lion

Seal

Penguin

**FALKLAND
ISLANDS
(U.K.)**

Cape Horn

The Mighty River

The Amazon, with the rivers that flow into it, is the world's second longest river. Its total length is about 4,000 miles, which is more than the distance across the United States. (The longest river is the Nile in Africa, 4,145 miles long.)

Beautiful Rio

Rio de Janeiro is a beautiful port city on the Atlantic coast of Brazil. Once a year, in February or March, the people celebrate Carnival with parades, fancy costumes, and dancing.

The Falkland Islands

This group of islands is east of Argentina. Many of the people raise sheep. Seagulls and penguins also live in the Falkland Islands.

11

Europe

Europe is part of the same land mass as Asia. It has many parts that are close to oceans and seas. The United Kingdom, Ireland, and Iceland are large island countries of Europe in the Atlantic Ocean. Norway, Sweden, Finland, and Denmark form a region called Scandinavia. Spain and Portugal make up Iberia.

The Land

Scandinavia has mountains, forests, and lakes. The mainland of Europe is a plain stretching from the Atlantic Ocean to the Ural Mountains. The highest mountains are near the Mediterranean and Black Seas.

The Weather

Near the Arctic Ocean the weather is cold. Near the Atlantic Ocean it is mild and rainy. Places near the Mediterranean Sea have hot, dry summers and cool, rainy winters.

The People

Many different peoples have lived in Europe over the ages. There are Slavs, Germans, and Celts. People have also come from Asia and Africa. Europe has many different languages.

250	500	750

MILES

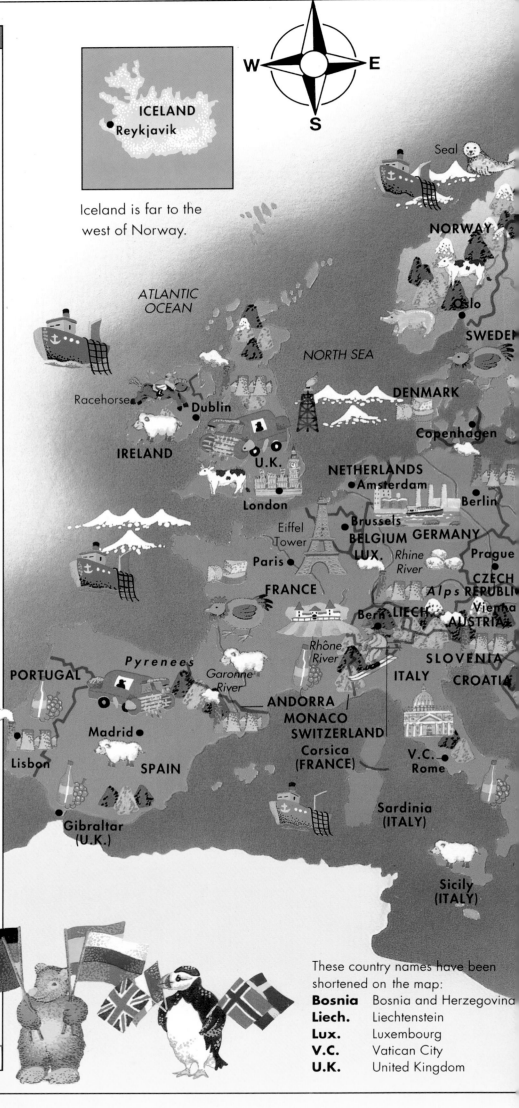

ICELAND
Reykjavik

Iceland is far to the west of Norway.

N
W   E
S

Seal

NORWAY

ATLANTIC OCEAN

Oslo

SWEDEN

NORTH SEA

Racehorse

Dublin

DENMARK

IRELAND

U.K.

Copenhagen

NETHERLANDS
Amsterdam

London

Berlin

Eiffel Tower

Brussels

BELGIUM GERMANY

LUX.

Rhine River

Prague

Paris

CZECH REPUBLIC

FRANCE

Alps

Vienna

Bern LIECH.

AUSTRIA

Rhône River

SLOVENIA

Pyrenees

Garonne River

ITALY

CROATIA

PORTUGAL

ANDORRA
MONACO
SWITZERLAND

Madrid

Corsica (FRANCE)

V.C.
Rome

Lisbon

SPAIN

Gibraltar (U.K.)

Sardinia (ITALY)

Sicily (ITALY)

These country names have been shortened on the map:

Bosnia	Bosnia and Herzegovina
Liech.	Liechtenstein
Lux.	Luxembourg
V.C.	Vatican City
U.K.	United Kingdom

Owl

Wolf

FINLAND

Brown Bear

Brown Bear

Ural Mountains

Helsinki

Tallinn

Stockholm

ESTONIA

Riga

LATVIA

LITHUANIA

Vilnius

BELARUS

Minsk

Moscow

RUSSIA

Volga River

Warsaw

POLAND

Oder River

Kiev

SLOVAKIA

UKRAINE

Iron Ore

CASPIAN SEA

Budapest

HUNGARY

ROMANIA

MOLDOVA

Dnieper River

GOSLAVIA

Danube River

Bucharest

BLACK SEA

Caucasus Mountains

Belgrade

BULGARIA

BOSNIA

Sofia

MACEDONIA

BANIA

GREECE

Athens

MEDITERRANEAN SEA

Reindeer and Snow

Lapp people live near the Arctic Ocean in Norway, Sweden, Finland, and Russia. Some keep herds of reindeer. Others live by fishing or farming.

St. Basil's Cathedral

This beautiful church is in the center of Moscow, the capital of Russia. It was built over 400 years ago. Its colorful domes are shaped like onions.

Big Ben

This big bell chimes out over London, the capital of the United Kingdom. Its clock tower is part of the Houses of Parliament, where British laws are made.

Ancient Greece

This great temple in Athens is called the Parthenon. It was built nearly 2,500 years ago. Many great thinkers, writers, and artists lived in Greece at that time.

Asia

Asia stretches from the frozen shores of the Arctic Ocean to the warm waters of the Indian and Pacific Oceans. It includes a large part of Russia as well as China and India. Asian cities are among the most crowded in the world.

The Land

Much of Asia is empty wilderness. There are huge pine forests and vast lonely deserts. Mount Everest, on the border between China and Nepal, is the world's highest peak (29,028 feet). Many people live in the broad river valleys of eastern and southern Asia.

The Weather

Parts of central Asia are bitterly cold in winter and scorching hot in summer. Winds from the Indian and Pacific Oceans bring heavy summer rains called monsoons to southern coasts.

The People

Asians were probably the first people in the world to farm, to build cities, and to use metal. Asia is home to Arabs, Chinese, Indians, Japanese, Jews, Mongols, Persians, Turks, and many other peoples.

| 500 | 1000 | 1500 |

MILES

Oil Wells

Countries in Southwest Asia have earned wealth by selling oil. The world's biggest oil field is in Saudi Arabia. Oil is also found in Russia and in China.

ARCTIC OCEAN

Ural Mountains

Ural River

KAZAKHSTAN

GEORGIA

ARMENIA

CASPIAN SEA

ARAL SEA

UZBEKISTAN

TURKEY

CYPRUS

LEBANON

ISRAEL

JORDAN

SYRIA

Baghdad

IRAQ

AZERBAIJAN

TURKMENISTAN

Tehran

IRAN

AFGHANISTAN

Indus River

KUWAIT

BAHRAIN

QATAR

U.A.E.

Riyadh

SAUDI ARABIA

OMAN

PAKISTAN

Sana

YEMEN

This country name has been shortened on the map:

U.A.E. United Arab Emirates

INDIAN OCEAN

Religious Beliefs

Many faiths began in Asia, including Islam, Hinduism, Buddhism, Judaism, and Christianity. Hindus worship at this temple in India.

N
W E
S

Polar Bear

Reindeer

Coal Mining

Lena River

RUSSIA

Brown Bear

Coal Mining

Trans-Siberian Railway

Lake Baikal

Siberian Tiger

Citrus Fruit

Ulan Bator

MONGOLIA

NORTH KOREA

Pyongyang
Seoul

JAPAN

Tokyo

Vegetables

Lake Balkhash Camel

Alma-Ata

Coal Mining

Beijing

SOUTH KOREA

KYRGYZSTAN Yak

TAJIKISTAN

Himalayas

lamabad

CHINA

Huang River

Yangtze River

Mount Everest

BHUTAN

Giant Panda

T'aipei
TAIWAN

New Delhi **NEPAL**

Bengal Tiger

HONG KONG
MACAU

PACIFIC OCEAN

INDIA

Hanoi

Manila

PHILIPPINES

BANGLADESH

Rangoon

LAOS

THAILAND

VIETNAM

MYANMAR (BURMA)

Bangkok

Cobra

CAMBODIA

Bananas

MALDIVES

BRUNEI

MALAYSIA

Kuala Lumpur

Orangutan

SRI LANKA

Colombo

SINGAPORE

INDONESIA

Jakarta

Modern Factories

Japan is famous for its factories. Japanese companies make computers, watches, televisions, radios, cameras, household goods, and cars.

Planting Rice

Over one billion people live in China. Chinese farmers must grow a lot of food. The main food of most of Asia is rice. It grows in flooded fields called paddies.

Africa

There are more than 50 countries in Africa. It lies between the Atlantic Ocean, the Mediterranean Sea, and the Indian Ocean. It is home to many animals, including elephants, lions, and crocodiles.

The Land

The Sahara is the world's biggest desert. In other parts of Africa are farms and rain forests. The highest mountain is Mount Kilimanjaro, which is 19,340 feet high. It towers over Kenya and Tanzania. The Nile, Niger, Zaire, and Zambezi are four of Africa's famous rivers.

The Weather

Many parts of Africa bake in the hot sun all year round. In other places there are months when it rains a lot, or months when it is windy and cool.

The People

Over a thousand different peoples live in Africa. They speak many different languages. There are big cities, but most Africans live in villages. Many Africans are farmers, growing crops or raising animals.

| 250 | 500 | 750 | 1000 | 1250 |

MILES

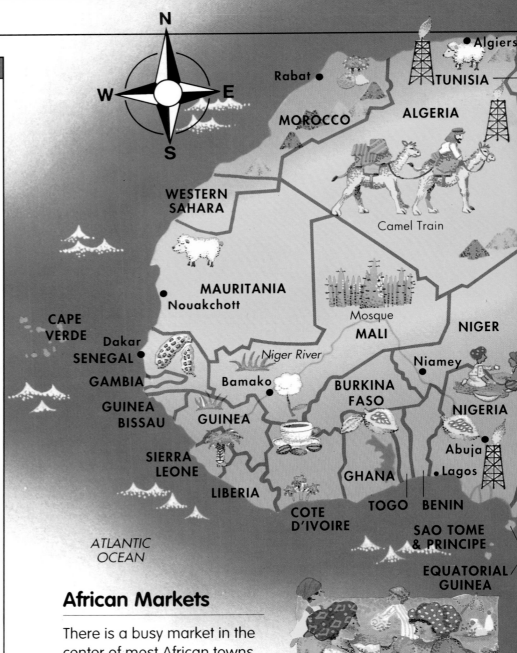

N
W E
S

Algiers
Rabat • TUNISIA
MOROCCO ALGERIA

WESTERN SAHARA

Camel Train

MAURITANIA
Nouakchott
CAPE VERDE
Dakar
SENEGAL Mosque
NIGER
MALI
Niger River
GAMBIA Niamey
Bamako BURKINA FASO
GUINEA BISSAU
GUINEA NIGERIA

SIERRA LEONE Abuja
Lagos
GHANA
LIBERIA TOGO BENIN
COTE D'IVOIRE
SAO TOME & PRINCIPE

ATLANTIC OCEAN
EQUATORIAL GUINEA

African Markets

There is a busy market in the center of most African towns. Farmers sell the food that they have grown. Others sell everyday needs like pots and pans, soap, and cloth.

River Transport

The Zaire River flows through thick rain forests. Many Africans use the river to travel. Some people paddle small canoes, while others go by river steamer.

Ancient Egypt

Thousands of years ago kings of Egypt built huge stone pyramids for their burial places. Nearby is a statue called the Sphinx.

African Wildlife

In parts of Africa there are still large herds of wild animals. On the grasslands are elephants, giraffes, and fierce leopards. Gorillas live in the forests.

Digging for Gold

In South Africa many people are miners. They drill into rock to dig out gold, iron ore, copper, and diamonds. The work is hard and dangerous.

Map labels:

nis
MEDITERRANEAN SEA
Tripoli
Mosque
Cairo
LIBYA
EGYPT
Sahara Desert
Oasis
Abu Simbel
Nile River
ERITREA
SUDAN
Khartoum
DJIBOUTI
Dhow
CHAD
N'Djamena
Chimpanzee
SOMALIA
Addis Ababa
ETHIOPIA
Baboon
CENTRAL AFRICAN REPUBLIC
MEROON
KENYA
Mogadishu
Zaire River
Gorilla
UGANDA
Kampala
CONGO
Lake Kivu
Lake Victoria
RWANDA
Nairobi
Mount Kilimanjaro
GABON
BURUNDI
Butterfly
ZAIRE
Giraffe
Dodoma
Dar-es-Salaam
Kinshasa
Cabinda (ANGOLA)
TANZANIA
INDIAN OCEAN
Luanda
Dhow
MALAWI
COMOROS
Lake Nyasa
Elephant
Lion
ZAMBIA
ANGOLA
Lemur
Lusaka
ZIMBABWE
Zambezi River
MADAGASCAR
Rhinoceros
BOTSWANA
MOZAMBIQUE
Antananarivo
Zebra
NAMIBIA
Zimbabwe Ruins
Walvis Bay
Windhoek
Gaborone
Pretoria
Maputo
SOUTH AFRICA
SWAZILAND
LESOTHO
Cape Town

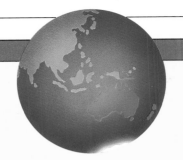

Oceania

This part of the world is called Oceania because it has many islands surrounded by oceans. The largest country is Australia. Near Australia are New Zealand, Papua New Guinea, and the Solomon Islands. Hundreds of islands are also scattered in the Pacific Ocean.

The Land

Australia's mountains are near the Pacific Ocean. Vast plains and deserts are in the middle of the country. Near the coast it is greener. New Zealand has green fields, hot springs, and mountains. Its highest mountain is Mount Cook. It is 12,349 feet high.

The Weather

The middle of Australia is hot and dry. The coasts have warm summers and mild winters. Papua New Guinea and parts of Australia are hot and wet. New Zealand is cool and mild all year.

The People

The first people in Australia were the Aborigines, and the first people in New Zealand were the Maoris. Later, many families from Europe and Asia came to live in this region.

| 250 | 500 | 750 | 1000 |

MILES

Ayers Rock

A huge red rock stands in the middle of Australia. It is 1,100 feet high. The local Aborigines believe that it is a holy place.

Darwin

Crocodile

INDIAN OCEAN

Iron Ore

Flying Doctor

Kangaroo

AUSTRALIA

Lake Eyre

Nullarbor Train

Lake Gairdner

Perth

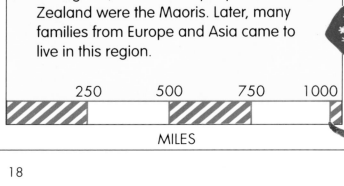

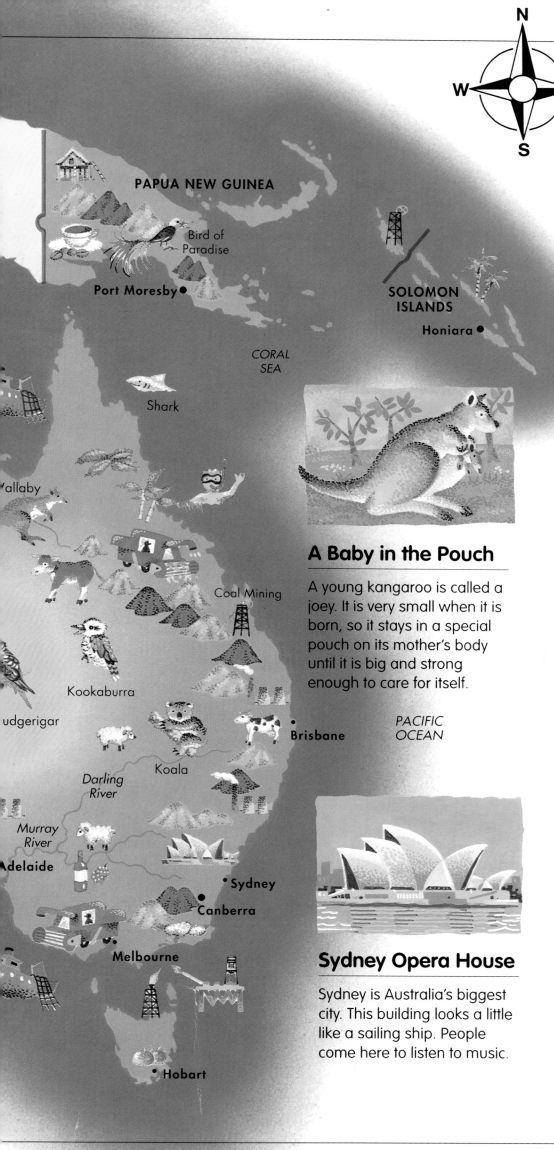

PAPUA NEW GUINEA

Bird of Paradise

Port Moresby

SOLOMON ISLANDS

Honiara

CORAL SEA

Shark

Wallaby

Coal Mining

Kookaburra

Budgerigar

Koala

Darling River

Murray River

Adelaide

Brisbane

PACIFIC OCEAN

Sydney

Canberra

Melbourne

Hobart

A House on Stilts

High stilts keep this house dry in one of Papua New Guinea's swamps. The country also has mountains and forests. Farmers grow crops and raise pigs.

A Baby in the Pouch

A young kangaroo is called a joey. It is very small when it is born, so it stays in a special pouch on its mother's body until it is big and strong enough to care for itself.

Baa!

Only 3½ million people live in New Zealand, but there are over 60 million sheep. Meat and wool from the sheep farms are sent all over the world.

Sydney Opera House

Sydney is Australia's biggest city. This building looks a little like a sailing ship. People come here to listen to music.

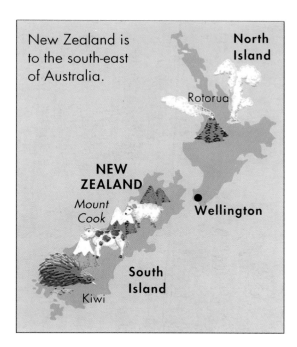

New Zealand is to the south-east of Australia.

North Island

Rotorua

NEW ZEALAND

Mount Cook

Wellington

Kiwi

South Island

The Arctic

The North Pole is the place in the world that is farthest north. It is at the center of the Arctic Ocean. It is covered by a thick sheet of ice. During the short summer, the edges of the ice melt. Huge chunks called icebergs break off and float away.

The Land and the People

The lands around the Arctic Ocean include Scandinavia, Greenland, Canada, and Russia. The Inuit of Canada hunt Arctic animals, and the Lapps of Scandinavia herd reindeer for a living.

```
   500    1000    1500    2000    2500
```
MILES

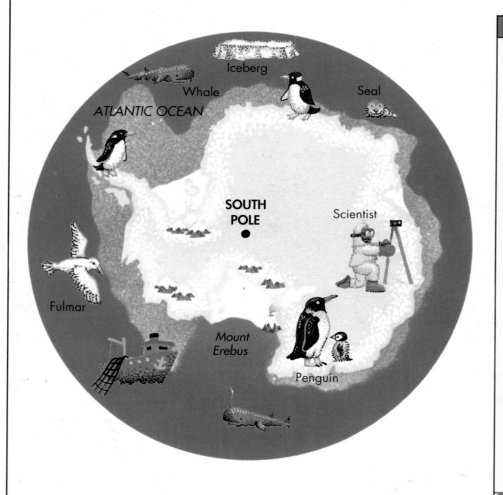

Antarctica

The place in the world that is farthest south is the South Pole. It is in a great continent called Antarctica. Antarctica is the coldest place on earth. Most of it is covered with ice and snow.

The Land and the People

Nobody lives in Antarctica. Scientists from all over the world have come there to work. They study the weather and the animals that live in Antarctica and the nearby seas.

```
   500    1000    1500    2000    2500
```
MILES

20